TABLE *of* CONTENTS

Light a match in a dark room and watch

as the light instantly overcomes the darkness.

Observe the power and grace of that single,

solitary flame dancing with life.

Now light several candles or kindle a fire and experience the added warmth and comfort extending from that first, vulnerable flame through others.

THIS IS THE HEART
AND SOUL
OF LEADERSHIP—
THE ESSENCE OF
INSPIRING OTHERS.

Leading with passion is about courageously casting off fear, doubt and limiting beliefs and giving people a sense of hope, optimism and accomplishment. It is about bringing light into a world of uncertainty and inspiring others to do the same. This is what we call passion, the fire within.

PASSION IS A HEARTFELT ENERGY THAT FLOWS THROUGH US, NOT FROM US.

It fills our hearts when we allow it to and it inspires others when we share it. It is like sunlight flowing through a doorway that we have just opened. It was always there. It just needs to be accepted and embraced. Under the right conditions, this "flow" appears effortless, easy and graceful. It is doing what it is meant to do. It is reminding us that we are meant to be purposeful. We are meant to be positive. We are meant to be passionate. We feel this when we listen to and accept our calling in life. We feel it as inspiration when we open the door of resistance and let it in.

Inspiration springs forth when we allow ourselves to be "in-spirit," aligned with our true essence. Stop and think about it:

When you feel truly passionate and inspired about someone or something, what frame of mind are you in? What are you willing to do? What kind of effort are you willing to put forth? How fearful are you? Chances are, you feel motivated to do whatever it takes, without fear or doubt, to turn your vision into reality. You grow in confidence. You believe you can do it. You are committed from the heart and soul.

10 ESSENTIALS *for* INSPIRING OTHERS

The purpose of this book is to clarify and offer ten key factors for leading with passion and inspiring peak performance.

These "essentials" serve to guide and remind leaders how they can "open the door" and facilitate flow. By practicing these essentials, you will tap the extraordinary potential in yourself and others and realize results you may never have dreamed possible. Look to any inspiring leader and you will see these key factors in action. Observe the best of the best and you will witness the power of passionate leadership. Make no mistake - leading with passion inspires world change. It is the only thing that ever really has.

USE THIS BOOK—
AND THESE ESSENTIALS—TO:

- Clarify purpose, context and meaning

- Create a compelling vision to focus intention and attention

- Gain commitment from the heart, not just agreement from the head

- Set priorities and focus efforts on what matters most

- Recognize and accept the power of grace

- Foster more creativity and innovation

- Demonstrate integrity and build trust

- Lead by passionate example

- Generate growth in yourself and others

- Awaken the Spirit in work

"Never doubt that a small group of committed people can change the world. Indeed, it is the only thing that ever has."

- MARGARET MEAD

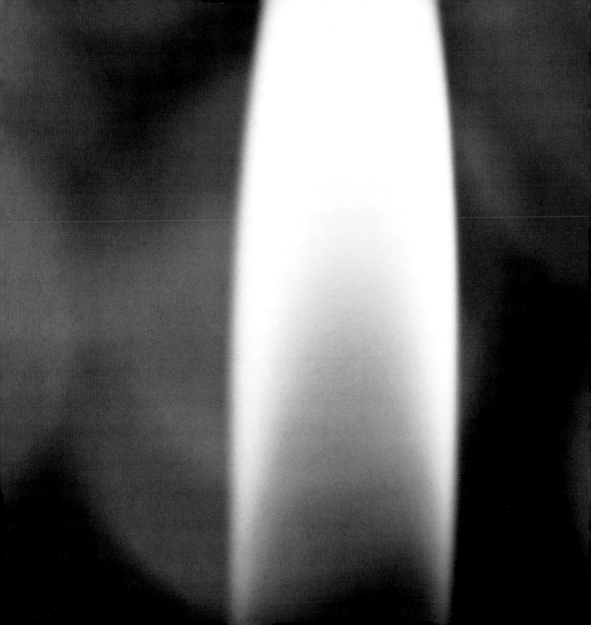

LEADING
WITH
PURPOSE

LEADING
with PURPOSE

How motivated are you when you have to do something without meaning, without purpose?

Have you ever been in a situation where you are loaded up with "content" but have no "context?" Perhaps it was a list of tasks you had to complete without any perceived value. Or maybe it was a complicated arrangement of activities with no emphasis on the connections holding them together, the "big picture." How motivating is this? Do you sometimes feel overwhelmed or "lost in the weeds?" After all, many people in leadership positions are far better at complicating things than simplifying them. Why is it that people tend to add to complexity rather than subtract what isn't needed?

"ANY INTELLIGENT FOOL
CAN MAKE THINGS
BIGGER AND MORE
COMPLEX... IT TAKES
A TOUCH OF GENIUS
- AND A LOT OF
COURAGE TO MOVE
IN THE OPPOSITE
DIRECTION."

—ALBERT EINSTEIN

Leading with passion requires that we lead with clarity and purpose, the simple elegance of meaning. To feel passion, we must be in alignment with reason. The reward must be in the work. We must relate with why we are doing what we are doing. We must understand the relationship between cause and effect, a systems perspective linking content with context. Purpose will drive the form, the details and the execution. Meaning will breathe life and motivation into the minutia. Strategy will inspire the tactics. But without a meaningful and compelling purpose, the fire of passion eludes us. We feel lost in a world of darkness, while others open the door to passion with a keen sense of meaning and purpose.

Leading with purpose begins with intention. Intention clarifies why we do what we do. Stop and ask yourself these questions throughout the day. Why do I do what I do? What is my intention? Does this intention move me? Does it stir my heart? Is it honest? Is it ethical? Will it make the world a better place? Take time to clarify your intention and contemplate your purpose. Listen to your heart and not just your mind when you do this. Does your purpose open the door to passion? Do you feel inspired by why you are doing what you are doing? If not, why not? What is missing? Why are you not in alignment? What happened? Why did you make this choice? What alternatives exist? Remember, passion exists all around us. It is like a specific frequency or channel on the radio. If we do not hear it or experience it, it does not mean it is not playing. It means we are tuned into something else. We are not in alignment. We are missing it.

Effective leaders know that a keen sense of purpose is very empowering. It elicits passion. It opens the door to this extraordinary energy of intuition, light and inspiration. Effective leaders also know that passion is contagious. It catches on. One lit match can light many candles. People feel the energy of passion.

They sense it. They are intrigued by it. Some are even awed by it. And those who have a shared sense of purpose will have a shared sense of passion. This trumps any carrot and stick incentives an organization can offer. The motivation coming from a shared sense of purpose and passion can literally move mountains. It

Lead with these gifts and
you will lead with purpose.

Lead with purpose and
you will lead with passion.

"I know of no more encouraging fact than the unquestionable ability of man to elevate his life by conscious endeavor."

- HENRY DAVID THOREAU

LEADING
WITH
VISION

LEADING *with* VISION

Purpose gives us meaning and context. Vision gives us clarity and direction. Together, these two leadership essentials inspire ingenuity and a compelling sense of desire.

We know what needs to be done. We can see it in our mind's eye. To illustrate the power of vision, imagine you are sitting blindfolded with a tinker toy model on a table in front of you, just out of reach. Your task is to reproduce the model in less than two minutes. You cannot touch the model, but you do have a supervisor who can provide you with limited feedback and you have all the supplies you need. Unfortunately, your supervisor has been instructed to provide you with negative feedback only! This is actually an exercise I use in a leadership development workshop, and this first round of the exercise is to demonstrate the disempowerment people experience when they cannot see the vision and they receive only negative, management-by-exception, feedback. Can you imagine how you might feel? You do not know exactly what to make and every time you grab the wrong part you are told "no" or "wrong." If you happen to grab the right part, you hear nothing at all. Not very inspiring, is it? Yet this simple demonstration represents the "disconnect" people all over the world frequently feel when the vision is not clear and they are not supported with positive direction and feedback.

Now let's try another round of the exercise. This time, imagine you are still blindfolded with two minutes to reproduce the model, but your supervisor can now provide you with positive feedback. In other words, if you grab a part you need, your supervisor will say "yes" or "right." Participants in this round generally report feeling much better about the task and the work environment, but there is still not much authentic spirit in the work. The clock winds down and no one gets it quite right. Progress has been made and confidence is higher, but performance is still weak. Some participants even ask for "more time," convinced they can get it right. More time and resources are a common response when people and organizations fall behind. We need more people! We need more capital! We need more capacity! We need more inventory! We need more time! The visionary leader challenges this common paradigm of scarcity by asking if there is anything obstructing our view. Is there anything constraining us? What might we do to facilitate better flow and understanding?

Cultivating a passionate and inspiring work environment requires clear and compelling vision that is shared by the team. It is simply not enough for one person to see the "desired state" and everyone else to guess at it.

TO INSPIRE PEOPLE,
THE PASSIONATE LEADER
MUST SHARE THE VISION
AND BE SURE IT IS CLEAR
AMONG CONSTITUENTS.
THIS SHARED VISION
HELPS CREATE A
COLLECTIVE MIND, A
CRITICAL BUILDING BLOCK
FOR HIGH PERFORMANCE
TEAMWORK.

Leading with a clear and compelling vision helps align team members with a sense of direction and focus. It gives the team something to aim at, something to make happen, something to manifest into positive results.

THIS MEANS THE LEADER MUST BE DELIBERATE AND VIGILANT IN ELIMINATING BARRIERS AND OBSTACLES, GIVING PEOPLE A KEEN LINE OF SIGHT.

This might range from hitting clear customer service metrics to reproducing a tinker toy model. In the example of the exercise, it is as simple as removing the blindfolds and showing people exactly what it is you want them to do. When we do this in a workshop, participants' first reaction is usually "Wow," followed by laughter, relief, a clear sense of purpose and focus and a finished model that meets or beats all expectations. In fact, we now realize that adding more time and resources was not the best idea. We had more than we needed to complete the task using a different paradigm. Where we thought there was scarcity, we discovered abundance. How about you? Can you see clearly what you need to do?

"Imagination is everything. It is the preview of life's coming attractions."

– ALBERT EINSTEIN

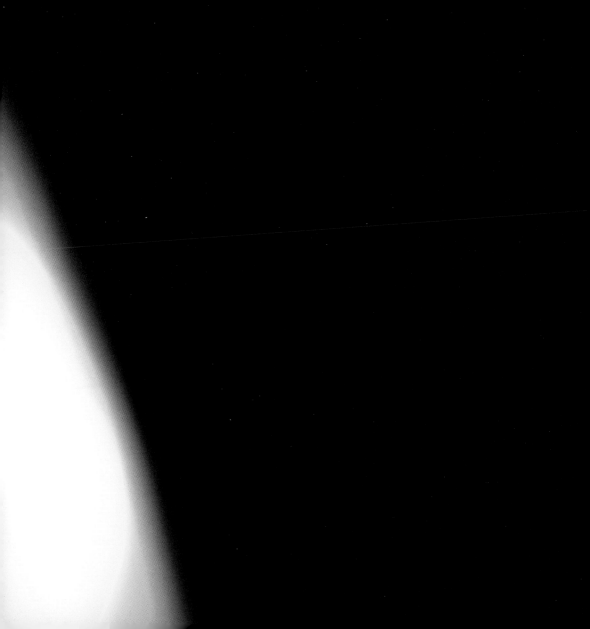

LEADING
WITH
HEART

LEADING
with HEART

There is no substitute for heart. It is the altar of spirit, the center for inspiration. One cannot fake authentic courage. Where there is doubt, there is disbelief. One cannot pretend to be compassionate.

These are qualities of the heart, not the mind. We use the mind to gather information, to analyze data and to draw intellectual conclusions. But it is from the heart that we build genuine relationships, bonds built with unconditional love, authentic joy, loyalty, trust and conviction. It is through the heart that we connect with the world around us, the people, by connecting at the level of the soul. With heart, we foster commitment, not just agreement. With heart, we defy the odds of logic and rationale. We experience true passion, fueling us beyond normal limits and building a sense of awe. With heart, we take risks, forgiving our-selves and others for mistakes and miscalculations along the way. With heart, we go first, leading the way.

THERE IS NO LIMIT TO THE HEART. ITS ENERGY IS UNIVERSAL. TIME AND TIME AGAIN IT EMPOWERS US TO MANIFEST PURPOSE AND VISION INTO EXTRAORDINARY RESULTS.

Leading with heart gives us the courage and fuel to do something with purpose and vision. Think of this like getting into your car to go to the grocery store. The vision is clear. You know where the grocery store is and you know how to get there. The purpose is clear. You want or need something from the store.

Otherwise, why waste your time and energy? Now you need the wherewithal to get there. You need fuel to move you forward, to help you accomplish your mission. With a full tank, you can get on your way without hesitation, building momentum as you go. But without heart, you feel distracted, defeated, discouraged and perhaps even dispirited.

EFFECTIVE LEADERS DO NOT ACCEPT THIS FEELING OF DEFEAT BECAUSE THEY KNOW HOW DISEMPOWERING IT IS. WITHOUT HEART, THERE CAN BE NO PASSION, NO ENTHUSIASM, NO FEELING OF ENERGY AND NO CHARISMA. A LEADER HIGH ON HEART AND EMOTIONAL INTELLIGENCE BREEDS VICTORY. A DISHEARTENED LEADER, DOUBTFUL AND STRESSED, MANIFESTS LOSS.

Stop and ask yourself from time to time: Is my heart in my work? Am I running on a full tank of energy? Do I lead with heart? Is this reflected in the people I surround myself with?

PASCAL ONCE WROTE,

"THE HEART HAS REASONS THAT REASONS CANNOT KNOW."

Perhaps this insightful statement helps us understand the nature of certain amazing discoveries, innovations, accomplishments and even miracles. One does not have to look far to read about, witness and experience the awesome power of heart. It is what makes the difference in the world today—as always. Look into any astonishing achievement and you will find someone leading with heart. Consider just for a moment the scientists, athletes, teachers, astronauts, healers, presidents, entrepreneurs,

politicians, social workers and leaders of all kinds who have made such a difference in the world as we know it. In many cases, these passionate leaders were not popular at the time. Some were even imprisoned, persecuted by the mainstream and put to death. Others were criticized, judged and cast aside.

But the leaders who made the greatest difference did it with heart. And with heart, there is no giving up. The heart has reasons that the mind knows nothing of.

"*What lies behind us and what lies ahead of us are tiny matters compared to what lives within us.*"

- HENRY DAVID THOREAU

LEADING
WITH
ATTENTION

LEADING
with ATTENTION

Leading with purpose, vision and heart is often not enough to efficiently get us to the top. As the old saying goes, "The devil is in the details." If we are not grounded in reality with good data, facts, information and feedback, we can easily misfire.

Passionate leaders are most effective when they know where they are and how they are doing. This means paying attention to the now. Start with an honest, candid look at the facts. What is your baseline assessment today? How long does it take to do what you do? What is considered benchmark quality and timing? What is considered best in class performance? How do you compare? Think of this like going in to see your doctor for a checkup. Start with a clear and measurable assessment of the current state, followed by some credible cause and effect analysis and benchmark standards. What is your blood pressure? What is your cholesterol level? What is your blood type? What are you eating and drinking? What are you doing for your body, health and overall well-being? Are you currently on any medications? What are they? What specifically is going on now? Patience is a virtue. Start by gathering the facts.

It makes little sense to spend time and energy trying to solve a problem that doesn't exist. It also makes little sense ignoring a problem that does exist or missing a problem because your mind is somewhere else.

THE ATTENTIVE LEADER LIVES IN THE NOW. EVEN WHEN REFLECTING ON PAST PERFORMANCE AND VISUALIZING FUTURE CHANGES, THE EFFECTIVE LEADER IS WORKING FROM THE ONLY TIME THAT REALLY MATTERS, THE ETERNAL NOW.

Consider a great athlete, musician, artist or surgeon. One of the most fundamental keys to success is their ability to focus on the immediate work at hand. Some call this the "zone." It is a mindful and heartfelt manifestation of flow. This is where everything comes together—purpose, vision and heart. We fully concentrate on what we have immediate command over. Whether it is hitting a golf ball, shooting a free throw, singing a song, painting a landscape or repairing a damaged body, we know we must be mindful of the present. A lapse in focus here can make a huge difference.

Passionate leaders also recognize the value in attending to people and relationships, not just tasks and assignments. At the end of the day, all tasks and assignments connect together in some way, and most have something to do with people. It is the relationships that we must always pay close attention to, not just the individual people and tasks. Accurate and efficient execution of tasks without efficient and effective relationships can well lead to failure.

W. EDWARDS DEMING, THE GRANDFATHER OF *TOTAL QUALITY MANAGEMENT*, ONCE SAID,

"PUT A GOOD PERSON IN A BAD SYSTEM AND THE BAD SYSTEM WINS. NO CONTEST."

If we, as leaders, do not attend to the systems people are using, we could be missing the real problem. This speaks to the vital relationship between tasks. The same holds true for people. According to multiple university studies on the impact of verbal communication, approximately 55 percent comes from body language and 38 percent comes from tone. This leaves only 7 percent for content—what is actually being said! If we pay attention only to content without attending to overall impact, we fall short of inspiring people.

THE ATTENTIVE, PASSIONATE
LEADER KNOWS THAT IT IS NOT
JUST WHAT I SAY TO PEOPLE, BUT
HOW I SOUND WHEN I SAY IT AND
WHAT I LOOK LIKE WHEN I SAY IT
THAT HAS THE MOST IMPACT.

INSPIRING LEADERS PAY ATTENTION
TO IMPACT AND THE CONNECTION
WE ALL SHARE. LEADING WITH
PASSION REQUIRES PAYING ATTENTION
TO WHAT MATTERS MOST!

"Things which matter most must never be at the mercy of things which matter least."

- JOHANN WOLFGANG VON GOETHE

LEADING
WITH
INTEGRITY

LEADING
with INTEGRITY

How can one speak of passionate leadership and inspiring others without including integrity? Integrity defines us by aligning who we really are—at the soul level—with how we behave at the human level. It is what others see in us as a reflection of what we see in ourselves.

When we are in harmony and balance with our core essence, our authentic self, we act with power, strength, confidence and grace. We feel whole and complete because we recognize we are whole and complete. There is no false self, no ego temptations, driving fear, guilt, greed, limiting beliefs or artificial pride in our behavior and actions. We think and behave with composure, humility, equanimity and a profound sense of inner peace. We are not seeking attention and approval from others. We know we are loved and cared for. We are not trying to manipulate or control people. We are honestly and genuinely pursuing what we know in our hearts is best for the greater good. This integrates us with life force energy, with Spirit, and with one another, giving us extraordinary power and grace. With integration comes synergy and teamwork at the most profound level.

With integrity, we experience life with the knowledge and wisdom of sage leaders. We know that we are never alone. We know that there is a reason for everything and a lesson within. We understand that we are not independent and separate from one another, but interdependent and connected. We are as one. We know that there are no idle thoughts, that what we think and what we feel has energy to it. We recognize the cause and effect nature of things and that what we sow is what we reap. We learn that what we attract into our lives is a reflection of how we think, feel and behave. Therefore, we realize that leading with integrity draws integrity into our lives.

Authentic teamwork requires trust, a cornerstone to any healthy relationship. Integrity builds trust, within oneself and with one another.

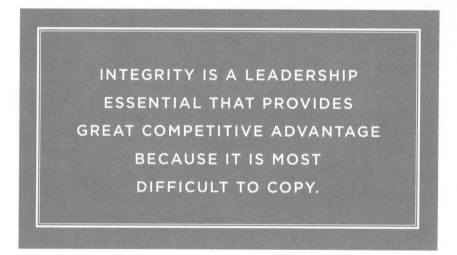

INTEGRITY IS A LEADERSHIP
ESSENTIAL THAT PROVIDES
GREAT COMPETITIVE ADVANTAGE
BECAUSE IT IS MOST
DIFFICULT TO COPY.

IT <u>CANNOT</u> BE FAKED
for integrity is honest and genuine.

IT <u>CANNOT</u> BE MANIPULATED
for integrity is steadfast and constant.

IT <u>CANNOT</u> BE DIVIDED
for integrity is whole and complete.

IT <u>CANNOT</u> BE TAKEN ADVANTAGE OF
for integrity knows no bounds.

IT <u>CANNOT</u> BE STOLEN
for sharing it makes it stronger.

IT <u>CANNOT</u> BE FOUGHT
for fighting it gives it power.

When we lead with integrity, we lead with spirit. We lead with authenticity. We lead with truth. Integrity gives us a direction and a compass so that we are never lost. It points the way to our true self.

Take time now to contemplate your integrity. Do you feel whole and complete, or does it seem like something is missing? What might that be? How did this come to be? What is it you might be resisting or pushing away? Are you walking your true inner talk? What is your inner spirit asking of you? What is your inner guidance system telling you? To what extent are you distracted by ego interference? How do you perceive others? How are you perceived by others? Do you see a correlation? Are you trusted? Are you trustworthy? Do you trust others? Do you lead by example, demonstrating integrity? Do you feel free?

After all,
INTEGRITY SETS PEOPLE FREE.

"*What you are thunders so loudly that I cannot hear what you say to the contrary.*"

- RALPH WALDO EMERSON

LEADING
WITH
DISCIPLINE

LEADING
with DISCIPLINE

Are you a disciple of action? When it comes to walking your talk, do you walk with responsibility and accountability? Do you execute your intentions with attention?

Leading with discipline requires motivation and effort. It is easy to say we are going to do something. It is quite another to let our actions speak for themselves. It is common to dream. It is less common to turn those dreams into something beneficial, something truly inspiring.

Leading with discipline requires initiative, action and stewardship. This means taking the required steps, doing the homework, working with others, committing to service and following through. It means accepting a certain degree of risk and sacrifice to challenge oneself and raise the bar.

Discipline means showing up early, staying late and doing whatever is ethically necessary to get the job done well and on time. Discipline means saying "no" to negative thinking and disempowering actions and saying "yes" to getting involved and being part of the solution. Discipline means going the extra mile, where there is typically less traffic.

When we act with discipline we demonstrate care, concern and dependability. We account for ourselves, our teammates and our results.

Leading with discipline requires setting goals and establishing measurement. With effective goals and metrics, we set expectations, assess performance and make adjustments as needed. Without access to the score, we lose the means to accurately measure performance against standards and evaluate progress.

Setting goals and keeping score is motivating. Consider any sport as an example. Without clear goals and scorekeeping, the sport can quickly lose momentum and enthusiasm. Often, it becomes boring. However, when a scoreboard lights up and the clock is ticking, the same physical requirements take on new meaning. Something within us lights up. We want to perform well. We want to set a new record. We want to do better than we did before. The simple act of setting goals and measuring performance is a powerful strategy for leading with passion and discipline. It triggers the heart as well as the mind.

Within every passionate leader is a deep sense of conviction. Goals are set to drive focus and accountability. Metrics are in place to assess balance and performance. Heartfelt commitment is embodied to fuel courage, initiative and action. There is a keen sense of discernment, responsibility and decisiveness. Work gets done on time. Good habits are formed. Bad habits are broken. Balance is maintained within and among tasks, activities and relationships, resulting in a sense of harmony and oneness. Think of this like conducting an orchestra. Without discipline, each functional unit could play at will, resulting in a great deal of noise. The passionate leader teaches the value of discipline, timing, practice, participation, patience, teamwork, measurement, and balance. Together, we can make beautiful music, but it does require discipline as an essential habit.

Take a moment now—a moment of discipline—to evaluate your own habits and tendencies. What do they tell you about your sense of passion and leadership? Are your actions inspiring? Do you finish what you start? Do you set clear, specific, measurable goals? Do you keep score, and if so what specifically do you track? Are you holding yourself and others accountable for performance? Are you stretching yourself and your team to rise to new heights? Are you identifying obstacles to peak performance and removing them? Are you pulling the weeds?

"A man's mind stretched to a new idea never goes back to its original dimensions."

— OLIVER WENDELL HOLMES

LEADING
WITH
GENEROSITY

LEADING *with* GENEROSITY

Wise, passionate leaders believe in abundance rather than scarcity. This means that the more we give, the more we have to give. In short, generosity generates abundance.

When we give with passion, we gain passion. When we offer an idea, we grow in creativity, retaining the original idea and expanding from it. When we give love, we are filled with more love to give. When we share our vision, we see more clearly as a team. When we teach, we learn. When we forgive, we are forgiven. When we offer peace, we feel peace. When we are generous with the heart, our heart grows stronger. We generate more love, passion, kindness, courage and conviction through the heart by exercising it. The same is true with the mind.

When we share our ideas, we enrich the mind. Inspiring others is a matter of giving abundantly, sharing what is meant to be shared and looking out for one another.

Leading with generosity is like tending to a garden. The objective is growth and prosperity. It is about transforming tiny seeds, like ideas, into healthy, nutritious plants and radiant flowers. It is about giving energy to gain energy. It is a cooperative, win/win effort. How can I help you help me? This requires that we are generous with our time, our resources and our attention. We must give of ourselves in order to receive. To obtain healthy growth, be it a garden, a team or an entire organization, we must appreciate, cultivate and nurture life in that environment. We must give of ourselves to manifest our vision and generate positive results. Challenges will come our way. Adversity will raise its testy head. Weeds will attempt to overtake our garden. But the passionate leader will quickly recognize the need for attention, integrity and discipline and act decisively. In order to generate more, the passionate leader minds these essentials with purpose, vision, generosity and heart.

Feelings of scarcity can distract the abundant mind with illusive logic and rationale like, "If we give, we no longer have." But the wise and passionate leader discerns truth from falsehood, recognizing that when it comes to what really matters, generosity generates! This knowledge comes from experience, not theoretical logic or philosophical debate. Just imagine how you might feel if you had a boss who looked out only for his best interest. Consider how you would feel if your feelings were not considered. Think about your thoughts when your thoughts don't seem to count.

WE ARE BORN TO GENERATE AND TO GENERATE,
WE MUST BE GENEROUS.

We must constantly ask ourselves, "What do I have to offer?" and "How can I give more?" When we fuel the law of abundance with heartfelt energy and inspiration, we inspire others. We experience abundance.

Give yourself a few minutes right now to contemplate the gifts you have to offer. Consider any special talents you have and skills you have developed. Think about time and attention, the intangibles as well as the tangibles. Ask yourself, "How can I make this world a better place?" You will find an abundance of answers. Then act on it! This is called leading with generosity, an essential to leading with passion.

"It is one of the most beautiful compensations of life, that no man can sincerely try to help another without helping himself."

- RALPH WALDO EMERSON

LEADING
WITH
CREDIBILITY

LEADING *with* CREDIBILITY

When it comes to influencing and inspiring others, nothing speaks louder than credibility. To truly inspire others, they have to want to do what you want them to do. They have to believe in you and the direction you intend to go.

This is not a matter of external force. It is a matter of internal motivation and empowerment. It is not a tactic of authoritative push. It is a strategy of magnetic pull. It is not an exercise in using command and control authority. It is a matter of using the power of suggestion and attraction. Leading with passion effectively requires leading with credibility.

To some, leading means "going first." We lead most effectively by example, by showing people the way. As Gandhi put it,

"Be the change you wish to see in the world." This requires a keen sense of self-awareness and insight on the part of the leader. We must be tuned in, highly conscious of our own intuitive guidance and behavior.

> *We must speak from a depth of knowledge,*
> *drawing from a rich pool of experiences,*
> *emotional intelligence and ingenuity.*
> *We must have extraordinary faith and belief*
> *in what we say and do and in what we*
> *intend to do in order for others to*
> *take the matter seriously. Without this depth*
> *of passionate belief, it is unrealistic to expect*
> *others to believe in our cause.*

SOME PEOPLE SAY,

"I will believe it when I see it."

THE PASSIONATE LEADER TRUSTS,

"I will see it when I believe it."

From deeply held beliefs come confidence, courage and conviction of the heart. This translates into passion, a contagious energy that speaks to people soul to soul. Belief breeds commitment and commitment cultivates passion. When Hannibal said, "We will either find a way or make one," people believed him because he had credibility, enthusiasm and conviction. He had a track record that showed he walked his talk. This was not an empty promise or a blind threat. It was perceived by many as a matter of fact.

When we lead with credibility and authenticity, we break through the denial and resistance of the ego. The passionate leader penetrates this self-limiting defense system—this sense of "knowing it all" pride—by providing information, knowledge, insight, context, revelation, epiphany, energy and enthusiasm that is difficult for people to ignore. It is as if someone shows up with a map and a light for a group lost in the dark. Yes, there will be some who insist on finding their own way without asking for direction or accepting the gift of light from someone else, but most people will recognize the value being offered and embrace it. Let's face it, credibility is essential in effectively parenting a child, teaching a student, healing the sick, building a team and showing people the way. It is a quintessential leadership characteristic. Credibility brings support to purpose and vision. It opens minds and hearts. It convinces people to accept and embrace change. It awakens the disempowered, shining light and hope on feelings of fear and despair. With credibility, all things seem possible. The light of passionate, credible leadership casts away shadows of doubt and disbelief. We find a way, or make one—without a doubt.

Now consider your credibility. Do people pay attention to you when you speak? Do they honestly believe what you say? Are they motivated and energized by your actions? Do they value what you have to offer? Do they see you as a positive role model and mentor? What evidence do you have to support your inquiries, comments, directions and requests? When you ask someone to do something, is it something you have done or would do yourself? Do you practice what you preach and preach what you practice? Are you the real thing in the eyes of the people you serve? Are you the example they want to follow?

"We are what we repeatedly do. Excellence, then, is not an act, but a habit."

- ARISTOTLE

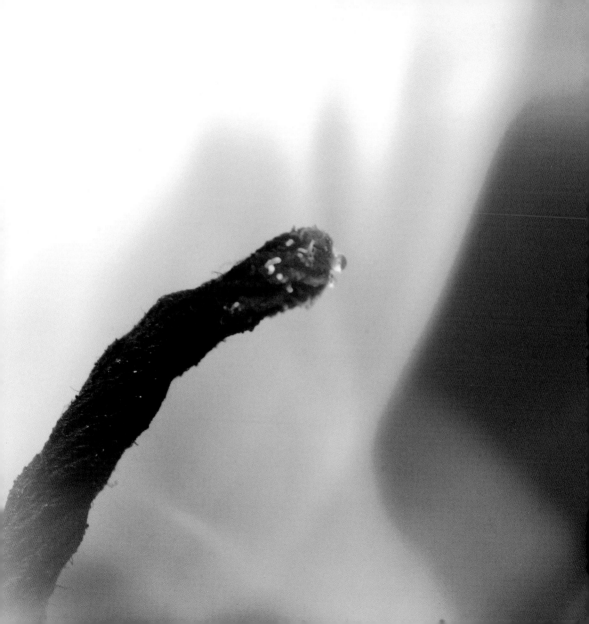

LEADING
WITH
GRACE

LEADING _with_ GRACE

Whenever we see a high performance team "in flow," we witness grace in action. We see what was referred to in ancient culture as Wu Wei, or effortless manifestation. We observe genuine alignment, appreciation, harmony and synergy.

It is like listening to a symphony. Personal agendas take a back seat and the ego thought system is transcended to a new realization. We are all one! We are all in this together. The all too common "Me-opic" perspective ("What's in it for me?") is replaced with "We-opic" vision, or "What's in it for we?" The power of one reveals itself to us and we feel awakened, alive, inspired and empowered. We experience a connectedness to one another, a collective mind and a heightened sense of appreciation. We gain confidence, openness, empathy, compassion and intuitive guidance. Worries and stresses melt away. Fear and doubts dissolve. Ideas flow and creativity expands. This symphony of coordinated, interdependent action is a reflection of leading with grace, an art not a science, a dance not a dictate, an essential to inspiring others.

In many ways, grace is ineffable. It is difficult to describe with words. Like the words love, appreciation, forgiveness and compassion, it must be experienced to be understood. People describe it in different ways, but the only way to know grace is to feel grace. Think of it as an energy field, surrounding, connecting and penetrating us. It touches us at the level of the soul, meaning that in order for us to lead with grace we must be humble and grateful. We must lead from the heart and soul with appreciation, dignity and respect. The brain and the intellect, while critically important to effective leadership, will not show us—or anyone else—true grace. We must go deeper than this, to the level where people "get the chills."

GRACE IS FLUID AND DYNAMIC,
WITH NO BEGINNING AND NO END.
IT IS ALWAYS PRESENT,
A FREQUENCY OR VIBRATION
THAT PLAYS CONTINUOUSLY—EVEN
IF WE ARE NOT TUNED INTO IT.

Think of it like soulful music playing on a continuous radio station. It is present whether we are listening to it or not. If we do not feel it, we are tuned into something else. We are not graceful by trying. A blade of grass does not try to grow green. It just does. We are graceful when we let go of our resistance to grace and align with its energy. This is of our core essence, beneath and beyond the ego thought system. To access it, we must release ego thinking—disempowering thoughts such as greed, doubt, selfishness, pride, guilt and fear—and embrace our higher self. There is no pretending to be graceful, as it requires honesty and integrity to shine forth. One cannot pretend to be honest. One cannot fake integrity. One cannot fool universal law. When we witness grace, it is not unusual to feel a sense of awe, a sense of reverence, perhaps even physical vibration and tingles. This is a connection with spirit, a moment of inspiration and revelation. Passionate leaders understand this. By being "in-spirit," they connect with the grace in and between others. This is a soul-to-soul relationship, a link that transcends time and space and awakens the spirit at work.

Stop and evaluate your leadership style. Are you calm and relaxed when leading people? Do they see you as a pillar of strength, a constant in a field of uncertainty? Do you make your work seem effortless? Do you appreciate everything you have? Do you lead with confidence, composure, equanimity and a deep sense of peace? Do people feel more relaxed, confident and empowered in your presence? Imagine this basketball scenario: You have called time out with one second to play. Your team huddles around you looking for direction and support. You are down by one point with possession of the ball. You have to score to win this championship game. Your team is looking at you. There is tension, anxiety and stress in the air.

DO YOU BOW TO THE
PRESSURE OR DO YOU RISE
ABOVE IT WITH GRACE?

WHAT EXAMPLE DO YOU
SET FOR YOUR TEAM?

"Appreciation is a wonderful thing; it makes what is excellent in others belong to us as well."

- VOLTAIRE

LEADING
WITH
SPIRIT

LEADING *with* SPIRIT

What is it that is so mesmerizing about inspiring, passionate leaders? Why is it that they seem so confident, poised and charismatic? In one word, it is spirit.

These leaders open themselves to spirit, an unbridled energy, pure and authentic, fearless and free. Spirit breathes life into death, hope into despair and courage into trepidation. It unites power and grace, health and vitality, creativity and innovation. Spirit lights the way to discovery, growth and on-going improvement. It is empowering and transformative in nature, morphing caterpillars into butterflies and dispirited victims into enlightened champions—if we let it. When we fully embrace spirit, we feel free. We feel safe. We feel whole and complete. We see things differently. What was once seen as a worry is now viewed as a new challenge. What could be considered a failure is now perceived as a lesson learned and a chance to rise again. Doubt turns into dare and there is no going back. Doors of adventure, entrepreneurship and creative expression open wide and we take risks we might otherwise avoid. With spirit we tap curiosity, boldness, assertiveness and confidence, critical elements to effectively leading change and inspiring people.

> PASSIONATE LEADERSHIP REQUIRES POSITIVE ENERGY AND POSITIVE ENERGY FLOWS FROM SPIRIT.

There is no negative energy flowing from spirit. The negative energy we perceive in the world is simply the denial of spirit. It is our resistance to that which is natural within each one of us that keeps spirit from flowing through us. We can learn to go with the flow, or we can choose to deny it for fearful, doubtful, defensive reasons. It is in the denial of what is positive, infinite and eternal—spirit—that we experience negative feelings and emotions. Passionate leaders let this resistance go. When we are leading with spirit, we approach each day with joy, enthusiasm and positive expectations. We are conscious of what we eat, what we drink, what we say and what we do. We are deliberate and mindful in our actions and reactions. We respond to stimuli by consciously "minding the gap" between cause and effect. We all have choice, an ability to respond differently to any given stimulus. We can respond subconsciously, as if in our sleep or on autopilot, or we can respond consciously with spirit and discernment. It doesn't matter what provokes us or "pushes our buttons," we have choice. *We can choose to react negatively with fear, attack, defense or retreat. Or we can choose to respond positively with hope, faith, optimism and creativity.*

Leading with passion and spirit requires that we remain positive, attracting positive energy into our lives and into the solutions we seek. Problems will always come and go. This is the nature of the universe, the yin and yang of a perfectly balanced system. However, there is no problem without a solution and the passionate leader always remembers this powerful truth. We are never given a challenge we cannot meet or a problem we cannot solve. This is what keeps life interesting. We grow in spirit when we rise to these challenges. We overcome fear by confronting it and letting it go. We feed our soul when we stop denying it food. At the beginning of each day, the passionate leader remembers that we are spiritual beings destined to create a better world by thinking positively and acting wholeheartedly. And at the end of the day, the passionate leader realizes that to inspire others, we must be in-spirit ourselves.

"*Our greatest glory is not in never failing, but in rising up every time we fail.*"

- RALPH WALDO EMERSON

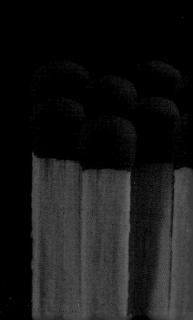

PUTTING
it all TOGETHER

A RECIPE FOR SUCCESS

People have debated for many years about the single most important characteristic or "ingredient" for leadership. These discussions tend to go on and on with interesting inputs but no resolution. The same endless debate might take place if we were to ask what the single, most important factor for chocolate cake is. Clearly, there is an argument for chocolate. There is also a good argument for eggs, flour, sugar, water and an assortment of other factors, including oven temperature and time in the oven. In fact, if any essential ingredient is missing or out of balance, the cake is vulnerable. It isn't everything it could be.

Effective, passionate leadership requires many things. In this book, we cover ten essentials. Combine these key factors and we have a means to inspire millions of people all over the world. These essentials transcend culture, race, gender, age, ethnicity and industry. They are a combination of ingredients that give leaders worldwide a means to bringing out the very best in people. Use them to tap the extraordinary power and passion available to you.

Start with purpose to make sure you are
doing what needs to be done.

Add a compelling vision to give people
something clear and meaningful to focus on.

Mix purpose and vision with heart to bind
with determination, courage and conviction.

Add a healthy amount of attention to be
present and aware of the now.

Blend with integrity to build trust and
demonstrate authenticity.

Bake with discipline to perform at optimal
levels and be accountable for results.

Cover with generosity so that
everyone gets a share.

Serve with credibility so that it tastes
as sweet as it is.

Give thanks with grace for the
abundance we have.

Enjoy with spirit and feed the soul.

 John J. Murphy is a highly recognized author, speaker and management consultant. Drawing on a diverse collection of team experiences as a corporate manager, consultant and collegiate quarterback, John has appeared on over 400 radio and television stations and his work has been featured in over 50 newspapers nationwide.

As founder and president of Venture Management Consultants, www.venturemanagementconsultants.com, John specializes in creating high performance team environments, teaching leadership and team development, and leading global kaizen events. He has trained thousands of "change agents" from over 50 countries and helped some of the world's leading organizations design and implement positive change.

John is a critically-acclaimed author and sought-after speaker. Among his other books are: *Pulling Together: 10 Rules for High Performance Teams, Beyond Doubt: Four Steps to Inner Peace, Reinvent Yourself: A Lesson in Personal Leadership, Agent of Change: Leading a Cultural Revolution, Get a Real Life: A Lesson in Personal Empowerment*, and *The Eight Disciplines: An Enticing Look Into Your Personality*.

The
simple truths®
DIFFERENCE

If you have enjoyed this book we invite you to check out our entire collection of gift books, with free inspirational movies, at www.simpletruths.com. You'll discover it's a great way to inspire friends and family, or to thank your best customers and employees.

For more information, please visit us at:

www.simpletruths.com

Or call us toll free... 800-900-3427